HUMAN BODY

Conceived and created
by Claude Delafosse
and Gallimard Jeunesse
Illustrated by
Pierre-Marie Valat

HIDDEN WORLD

A FIRST DISCOVERY BOOK

SCHOLASTIC INC.
New York Toronto London Auckland Sydney
Mexico City New Delhi Hong Kong

You cannot see inside your body, yet it is a fascinating universe.

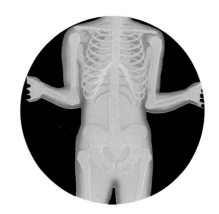

With this book, you will be able to observe your body as if it were transparent.

As you explore the pages of this book, a simple paper flashlight will reveal the world inside the human body.

Remove the paper flashlight from
the back of the book.

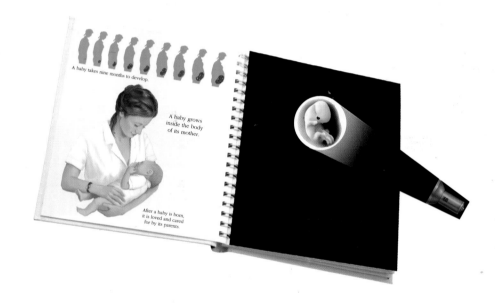

A baby takes nine months to develop.

A baby grows
inside the body
of its mother.

After a baby is born,
it is loved and cared
for by its parents.

Move the flashlight between the black pages
and the plastic pages to discover hidden images.

You hear with your ears.

You taste with your tongue.

There are five senses: hearing, taste, sight, smell, and touch.

You see
with your
eyes.

You smell
with your
nose.

You touch
with your
skin.

Because your bones are connected by joints, you can move them separately.

joint ▲

As you grow, your bones lengthen.

Hidden beneath your skin and muscles is the framework that allows you to stand and move: the skeleton.

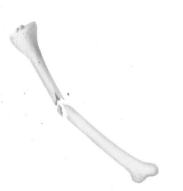

When a bone breaks, it must be held together until it has healed.

The Statue of Liberty has a "skeleton" made of iron.

To see
skeletons,
doctors use
X rays.

When you look at parts of the body under a microscope, you discover an extraordinary world.

A microscope makes very tiny things appear larger.

White
blood
cells

A
section
of skin
with a hair

Red blood
cells

Striated
muscle

Bone

Brain
cells

Egg
and
sperm cells

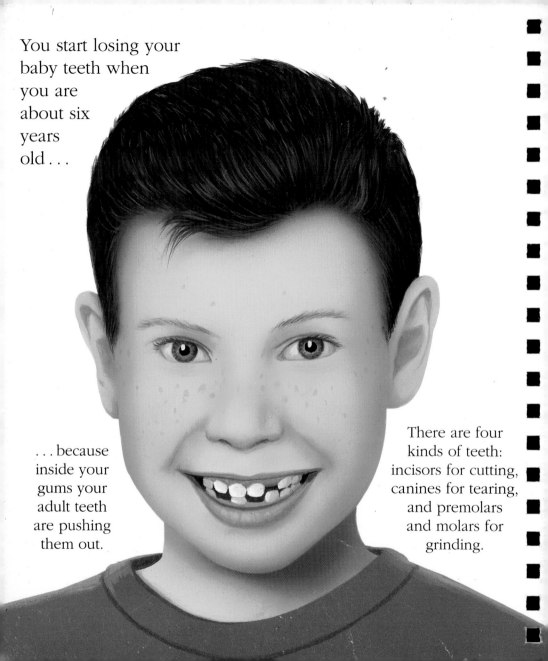

You start losing your baby teeth when you are about six years old . . .

. . . because inside your gums your adult teeth are pushing them out.

There are four kinds of teeth: incisors for cutting, canines for tearing, and premolars and molars for grinding.

 chew  swallow  digest  absorb eliminate

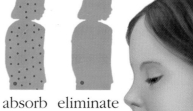

When you eat, your
food takes a long trip
inside your body,
traveling through your
digestive system.

These parts of the body
help you digest food:
1. esophagus
2. liver
3. stomach
4. gall bladder
5. pancreas
6. small intestine
7. large intestine
8. rectum

In the mouth, the sandwich is ground by the teeth and broken down by saliva. It then descends into the esophagus and the stomach, where it is broken down even more. Then it passes into the small intestine. The nutrients that are needed are absorbed by the body. What is left over travels into the large intestine and out the rectum.

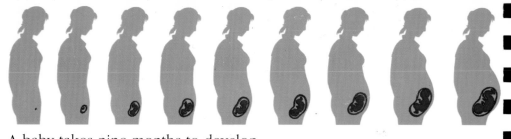

A baby takes nine months to develop..

A baby grows
inside the body
of its mother.

After a baby is born,
it is loved and cared
for by its parents.

**The fetus at
one month**

at a month
and a half

at three
months

at five months

You look a little bit like your mother
and a little bit like your father.

You may have
blue eyes
and straight
chestnut hair...

or brown eyes and
straight brown hair

or blue eyes and
curly red hair

or blue eyes and
wavy blond hair

...and there are many other wonderful possibilities.
Heredity is the transmission of characteristics
from one generation to another.

Sometimes certain characteristics skip a generation, so you may resemble your grandparents.

paternal grandfather

paternal grandmother

maternal grandfather

maternal grandmother

father

mother

From whom did these three brothers inherit their characteristics?

During sleep the body rests,
but the brain continues to be active.
Sometimes thoughts are transformed
into dreams or nightmares.

Although we may have different hair, eyes, skin, or shapes . . .

. . . on the inside we are all the same.

Did you find these hidden images . . .

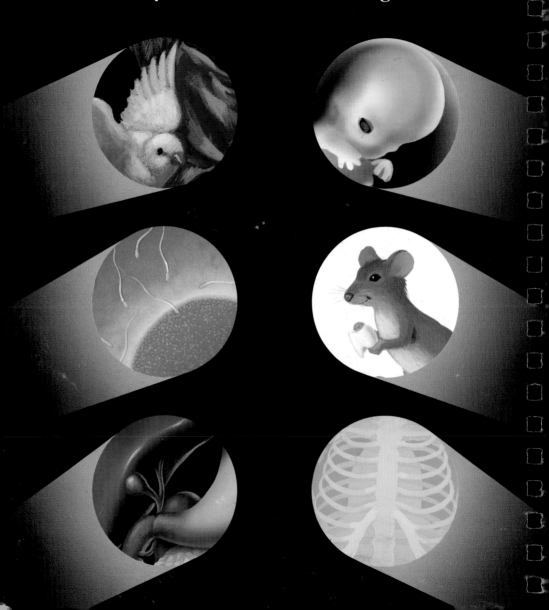

...with your magic paper flashlight?

Library of Congress Cataloging-in-Publication Data available.

Originally published in France in 1998 under the title *J'Observe: le corps humain* by Editions Gallimard Jeunesse.

ISBN 0-439-10681-8

Copyright © 1998 by Editions Gallimard Jeunesse.
This edition English translation by Mary Varilla Jones. Copyright © 2000 by Scholastic Inc.
This edition American text by Mary Varilla Jones. Copyright © 2000 by Scholastic Inc.
This edition Expert Reader: Dr. Ann-Judith Silverman, Department of Anatomy and Cell Biology, Columbia
University, New York, NY.

10 9 8 7 6 5 4 3 2 1   00 01 02 03 04

Printed in Italy by Editoriale Lloyd
First Scholastic printing, March 2000